Winter Wonderland

Echoes Of Winter

Edited By Roseanna Caswell

First published in Great Britain in 2024 by:

Young Writers
Remus House
Coltsfoot Drive
Peterborough
PE2 9BF
Telephone: 01733 890066
Website: www.youngwriters.co.uk

Book Design by Ashley Janson

Softback ISBN 978-1-83565-427-9
Printed and bound in the UK by BookPrintingUK
Website: www.bookprintinguk.com
YB0590BZ

Foreword

Dear Reader,

Welcome to Winter Wonderland, a showcase for our nation's most brilliant young poets to share their thoughts and feelings during the coldest months of the year. This collection covers every aspect of wintertime alongside deeper explorations of emotions and the topics that are important to them.

Young Writers was established in 1991 to nurture creativity in our children and young adults, to give them an interest in poetry and an outlet to express themselves. Seeing their work in print will encourage them to keep writing as they grow and become our poets of tomorrow.

Selecting the poems has been challenging and immensely rewarding. The effort and imagination invested by these young writers makes their poems a pleasure to enjoy reading time and time again. I hope you enjoy reading them as much as we did.

Contents

Aaron Lomas (10)	180
Valentina (10)	181
Noah Tuppenney (11)	182
Samuel C (10)	183
Henry (10)	184
Lizzie Webb (11)	185
Eren K (10)	186
Joshua Lindsay (11)	187
Jacob Banas (10)	188
Ebony Marlow (11)	189
Ronnie Bolton (9)	190
Lewis P (11)	191
Jasmine Cook (10)	192
Darcy Normington (10)	193
Lewis Robins (9)	194
Niamh Nichols (10)	195
Constance Prentice (9)	196
Lenny Davies (10)	197
Zoyia Zaidi (10)	198
Poppy Collins (10)	199
Klevis (10)	200
William (10)	201
Gabriella Rhoades-Brown (9)	202
Robyn Lyne	203
Rosie Somers (11)	204
Zac (9)	205
Bobby-Ross Doyle (9)	206

The Poems

Aged Reflections

Beneath the winter moon so bright,
Kids step on barren leaves in delight.
Stars are bathed in soft moonlight,
As my wise heart views this dead sight.

It doesn't feel like I've lived
In winter's chill, a solitary silence,
A frozen world where shadows creep:
Memories linger, as thoughts run deep.

It doesn't feel like I've lived
Yesterday dissolves in blurry mist,
Leaving me pondering to what I've missed.

It doesn't feel like I've lived
Fellow elders gaze upon the snow,
Reflecting on how the time did go.
At 84, in my armchair, mind as such,
Unable to escape this mental crutch.

It feels like I've lived, a lifetime adrift,
Captured in the four walls of philosophy.
When did all this 'time' leave?

Alex Marcu (16)
Archbishop Ilsley Catholic School, Acocks Green

The Festive Season Is Soon Approaching

The festive season is soon approaching
Winter weather might be better
The magical snow season
But don't worry, this holiday will sweeten
White snow falling to the ground
I start to worry, what is that sound?
Father Christmas will hand out presents
Naughty or nice?
Presents or coal?
Given to the perfect souls
As cold as an earthworm, the snow drifted
Santa will come, don't you miss it!
Ballerinas dancing in the sky
Children will start to cry
Elves give out presents from time to time
On Christmas, everybody should be fine
One reindeer has a big red nose
Another traditional thing is mistletoe
Each Christmas we start to grow.

Noor Fatima Khalid (9)
Bankfoot Primary School, Bradford

The Snow Fox!

Snow fox, snow fox
White and bright
Makes everyone feel alright.

With each step, the deep snow crunches
beneath his feet.
Waiting for the right time to devour, eating
his meat.

After he's done, he'll go out.
His rough paws trot on thick snow like a horse.

He uses all his force to dig, and get to his burrow,
Waiting for tomorrow.

Tomorrow is here, he likes to cheer
Waiting for the perfect deer.

Amaani Younis (9)
Bankfoot Primary School, Bradford

New Year

Fireworks exploding like bombs
The final countdown is over
Time is over for the New Year
Fireworks shooting in the air
Smell the smoke from the fireworks
It's a joyful time at midnight
The cool crisp air blew away
Hear my family shouting
"Happy New Year!"
This festival is enjoyable for everyone
My family are overjoyed at this festival
This cold festival is old
No homework today
Only fireworks this day.

Rayyan Sarwar (10)
Bankfoot Primary School, Bradford

Snow Wolf

S now slowly falling on my black coat
N o one wants to touch the enormous dog
O n the snow, the wolf howled and growled
W hilst the wolf was asleep, the glistening snow
fell on him.

W hen its prey sneaks away, the wolf stays hungry
all day
O n the snow was an unstoppable, untouched
pack of wolves
L ike a dog, it is fast and fearless
F rosty and icy make it slippery when it is sleepy.

Mohammed Ahmed (9)
Bankfoot Primary School, Bradford

Ice In Disguise

Ice could be nice but it is really cold,
It could be disguised into gleaming gold,
On the stage, feeling confident and bright,
Through the stars, giving everyone a fright!
Outside of the curtains, being their model,
As they watch other objects and animals waddle,
In the air, leaping as high as a kanga!
You could see more of me but not in Sri Lanka!
See me again on this day, December.
Today was a miracle, just to remember...

Areeba Shafiq (10)
Bankfoot Primary School, Bradford

White Tiger

W hite as snow
H igh amount of snow will grow and grow
I ntensely soaring leaving people shocked
T he snow left all the cars blocked
E veryone just keeps their doors locked.

T he elegant tiger strolling through the land
I nspecting the tiger that looks like white sand
G oing to its prey
E very other animal refuses to stay
R oaring over and over again.

Muhammed Khan (9)
Bankfoot Primary School, Bradford

Snow Owl

Snow owl, snow owl, snow owl,
It prowls at night and likes to fight
He waits for his prey
And lights the night
The snow under his feet crunches like meat
He goes into the tree
And likes to tweet
A few minutes later, he's fast asleep
He wakes up to hunt his prey
And goes back to keep it safe
Like a lion, the owl prowls
Waiting for the perfect time
To sing a winter song.

Aaminah Hameed (9)
Bankfoot Primary School, Bradford

Snow Wolf

S oft whispering snow in the night.
N o one wants to touch the wolf.
O n the snow, the wolf howled.
W hen it was night, the wolf slept.

W hen it saw its prey it sprinted after it.
O n the snow, the wolf was with its pack.
L ong and crazy, whatever, it doesn't care.
F rosty wolf glistens in the dazzling sky.

Muhammad Hadi Kamran (9)
Bankfoot Primary School, Bradford

Snowflakes

S nowflakes float down gently
N ear the pavement, so frozen and bare
O cean and river it will flow to
W aves shall roll to the shore
F alling from the sky
L ike soft cotton wool
A mazing cool air
K een night is dark with snowflakes
E veryone loves the snow.

Aryaan Afzal (9)
Bankfoot Primary School, Bradford

Snow Angels

The snow angels gracefully began
Dancing on the frosty clouds.
After every step, it was like
Crushing icicles beneath my feet.
Crunch, crunch, crunch
Like leaves falling from trees in the breeze,
The snowflakes settled with a fleet.
The snow started soaring in the silent spot.

Angela Zheng (10)
Bankfoot Primary School, Bradford

New Year

N ew year, new me, new learning
E verything will be a memory
W elcome the New Year while fireworks roar

Y ears to think, years to remember
E verything will come to an end
A miracle to see
R emember to keep happy and enjoy this year!

Abdullah Ayub (10)
Bankfoot Primary School, Bradford

Snow

The slushy, crunchy snow soaring down
Whispering like someone reading in a library
Gently but slowly the punch makes you poorly
Everything is so white, so bitter
I hear snow coming down
Swifting and drifting like race cars speeding down
But there is no noise.

Sufyaan Ali (9)
Bankfoot Primary School, Bradford

Snow

S now softly falls on my head like a bed, like
snowdrops in the sky
N o one comes out because it's cold
O h, why do you come in the evening?
W ith each step, the frosty snow crunches loudly
beneath my feet.

Amelia Shafiq (9)
Bankfoot Primary School, Bradford

Fireworks

Fireworks flying through the sky
As fast as thunder
Falling through the sky
Pop, pop, pop
Beautiful little
Spark, spark, spark
In the night
Laughing in the sky
As slow as snow
The fireworks go.

Noor Kauser (9)
Bankfoot Primary School, Bradford

Snowballs

The ice is cracking as we speak.
Snow is falling very deep.
I am really cold in the snow.
Ice is slippy, I'm slipping on my toe!
The wind is blowing round and round.
My favourite weather is winter,
Because I just love snowball fights!

Annalia Watling (6)
Bede Community Primary School, Gateshead

Snow

My name is Snow!
I am falling around the big trees.
There are no bees around.
The ice is cracking, and sharp pieces are falling
Fast into the soft snow below.
The fast snow is blowing through the trees.

Andrei Popa (7)
Bede Community Primary School, Gateshead

Winter

In the winter I play on a sledge.
The ice is slippery,
I wear my Christmas jumper to keep me warm.
My sledge speeds down the hill.
I feel the snowflakes fly up and land on my face.
I like winter!

Beni Botuna (7)
Bede Community Primary School, Gateshead

Winter

We make snowmen in the winter.
The snow is freezing cold, and the ice is slippery.
Snow falls from the sky
And freezes fast as it comes to the ground.
We make snowmen in the winter.

Matthew Robinson (8)
Bede Community Primary School, Gateshead

Winter

It is winter and it is very cold outside!
The snow is freezing and it covers my feet.
My wellies keep my feet dry.
I love the snow in winter,
Even when it is very cold outside!

Lincoln Christie (7)
Bede Community Primary School, Gateshead

The Cold Winter

It is cold in winter!
It is cold in the soaking, wet snow!
I wrap up warm, so I can play outside.
I like to play with my friends in the snow.
It is cold in winter!

Joey Fang (9)
Bede Community Primary School, Gateshead

Snow

When I go out, I put on my coat.
When I go out, I play with Miss Fenwick!
We play with lots of snow.
I like to play in the snow with Miss Fenwick!

Gerard Alvarado Romero (9)
Bede Community Primary School, Gateshead

Snow

Snow falls from the sky.
Oh, snow is sad but I feel alive!
Snowballs are fun!
I like the snow.
I feel happy in the soft snow.

Logan White (6)
Bede Community Primary School, Gateshead

Winter

In winter I feel cold.
This is good!
In winter I see Santa.
I see snow
And I see dancing snowflakes!

William Fearon (6)
Bede Community Primary School, Gateshead

Winter

In winter, it is very cold,
In winter, it is slippy,
In winter, it's freezing and my fingers tingle.

Riley Massey (8)
Bede Community Primary School, Gateshead

On A Crisp Winter's Night

On a crisp, winter's night,
Crystallizing fallen leaves, crunchy and light.
There lay a frosty sheet, covering the grass, freeze,
A blanket of dust hugging lonesome twigs
of bare, frozen trees.

Above me, emerged Sirius, to guide the way,
Glistening against the sky,
the stars come out to play.
Shining through the deep, dark abyss,
hanging high like a kite,
Encrusting the night, bejewelled
and bright, echo of light.

Last year swiftly passed like the breeze,
What lies ahead, what moments shall we seize?
A new year is now upon us,
opportunities gleam and glow,
Hope for seeds of pleasure. health and love, grow.

A bold robin, singing in as the moon beams,
While I'm walking through

the Winter Wonderland of dreams.
Silhouette of nature, enjoyed,
embraced, fresh, forgiving,
Thankful for the Evergreens, stags
and snowdrops, living beings.

Wrapped up, warm and toasty by the fire,
The gift of rest and warmth is a delightful desire.
Presents unwrapped, nothing under the tree,
embers still twinkling,
Food plentiful and roasted, candlelight of love
forever sparkling.

On a crisp winter's night,
With a brand new flame, I set the fire to ignite.
I hold the sense of safety, warmth and thanks,
The past, the present and the future reveal a path,
I step in, happy and gleeful.

Robyn Jones (11)
Bridgewater High School, Appleton

Christmas

C an you hear the sleigh bells ringing?
H appy sounds of children singing,
R eindeer fly in the moonlit night.
I t's time for bed, to be tucked up tight.
S anta's merrily on his way,
T oys are piled up on his sleigh.
M iles and miles
A round the world
S anta brings presents to boys and girls!

Pollyanna Tovey (11)
Bridgewater High School, Appleton

All Thanks To The Reindeer

On the night of Christmas Eve, so still and bright,
Santa Claus climbed into his sleigh with delight.
He called out, "Ho, ho, ho!" as he took flight,
With presents for every girl and boy in sight.

But disaster! As he flew over the town,
His sleigh suddenly came crashing down!
The reindeer were shaken and their antlers
were soaking.
As all the gifts and toys were broken.

Just when hope seemed lost that night,
A voice just spoke up with great might.
"I can help you, it's not tragic,
I can fix it with my magic!"

And so, Rudolph the Red-Nosed Reindeer,
Fixed the sleigh without any fear
The rest of that night, the sleigh did not fall,
And delivered to children big and small.

So, if you woke up to presents on
Christmas morning
And the day was still dawning.
Then it was all thanks to the reindeer,
Who fixed the sleigh when hope wasn't near.

Myles McNulty (8)

Broomlands Primary School, Kelso

Out The Window

Out the window,
That one morning,
The shock of the white floor,
The whitest floor you've ever seen,
The white floor that your grandparents
once talked about,
The white floor they call snow?

I had never seen snow before,
The white powder,
The white fluffy object,
The white fluffy object that just appears,
The white powder that is magic
The white powder that is called snow.

The white powder brought by Santa,
Brought by Santa as a gift,
A gift,
A gift that's rarely given,
The gift that creates its own world,
The white fluffy world.

The world only seen in movies,
The world dreamt about,
The world we thought was gone,
The world we thought was destroyed,
The world which was just hidden,
The world which is magic.

The world,
The world which exists,
The world which we thought was lost,
The world we thought would never come back,
Snow,
Snow is here,

Snow,
We thought we lost it,
We thought we would never see,
We get to see,
We get to see though our kids won't.
Snow is here.

Charlie Thomas (14)
Bruern Abbey Senior School, Chilton

Christmas

C hristmas is here
H ouses packed with Christmas cheer
R eindeer zooming in the air
I nside, elves are making fluffy teddy bears
S tockings have been packed
T oys under the tree were wrapped
"M erry Christmas!" Santa said
A s all the kids slept in their little beds
S oon kids will wake up to ride on their sleds.

Rudy Richards (14)
Brynteg Comprehensive School - Lower School, Bridgend

Wintertime

A cold and dreary night by the fire.
Talking and sipping hot chocolate.
Feeling cold-blooded like a vampire.
Everyone is tired and exhausted.

The snow continued for days
Christmas was a few days away.
We prayed for the day always
The further it was, the longer we pray

Winter is a time of joy
Coming together and having fun
With the ones that you love.
Both old and young.

Zikorah Anadu (12)
Campsmount Academy, Norton

Winter Nights

Winter bliss of night,
Inevitable risk of frostbite,
Snow coating like a warm blanket,
Taken by the cold like a bandit,
Leaves crunching underneath boots,
As the winter love aims to seduce,
Frozen hearts to love winter nights,
Help me look upon these sights.

Molly Laverick (13)
Campsmount Academy, Norton

My Elves

Jingles and Jolly, our elves so bright,
Visit us each year, one December night.
The best elves we have ever known,
Their love and magic, to us they have
always shown.

But when the last day of the year is near,
Back to the North Pole, they must steer.
A hug for their reindeer, Sven, we save,
He is the best reindeer, so happy and brave.

Every year, they are such a treat,
We make our Christmas cookies,
That are ooooh so sweet.

My sister and I, with hearts so light,
Write letters to Santa, in the moonlight.
Jingles, Jolly, and Sven's arrival, we adore,
But when they leave, our hearts feel sore.

Yet, Christmas is the reason for the season,
It is a time of love, joy, and reason.

Though Jingles, Jolly, and Sven depart,
Their Christmas spirit remains in our hearts.

Jamie Poole (11)
Caterham High School, Clayhall

Winter Wonder

W et, wispy winds start to travel through the skies,
I cing on the cake and extra mince pies.
N o one can wait, holidays are so very near,
T he families are gathering for festive cheer.
E arly nights are upon us, darkness fills the sky,
R acing down the snowy hills, lifting your hands up high.

W atching kids play with snow in the park.
O h, what a joy this season is, even in the dark.
N aughty or nice, only Santa knows.
D on't forget to listen out on Christmas Eve for his ho, ho, ho's!
E ven though this year is coming to an end,
R esolutions for the new year ahead, make sure to do one and tell a friend!

Imaan Allybaccus (12)
Caterham High School, Clayhall

Winter

W here snowflakes fall, creating a beautiful scene.
I cicles glisten in the pale moonlight,
N estled by the fire,
T he cosy warmth feels just right.
E agerly awaiting the first snowfall,
R oasting marshmallows, we hear them call.

In winter's embrace, we find delight,
Nurturing moments, so pure and bright.
So bundle up tight, let's go for a sleigh ride,
Laughing and smiling, side by side.
In winter's wonderland, memories we'll make,
Never wanting this enchanting season to break.

Lara Kaur (14)
Caterham High School, Clayhall

Winter's Festive Embrace

Deep in the quiet of winter's night,
Amongst the glow of the twinkling light,
Snowflakes sway in a graceful flight,
As Christmas approaches with pure delight.
Flares crackling with a snuggly hum,
Filling the air with warmth and joy,
Families write with life strums,
Below the tree, presents lay.
Christmas carols chanting through the air,
Increasing delight beyond compare,
The spirit of devotion floating in the sky,
Christmas magic twinkles in the air,
Painting joy everywhere.

Zainab Baig (11)
Caterham High School, Clayhall

Christmas

Up in the sky, up so high,
There was a star
So bright,
Little snowflakes dancing on my head,
All while I look ahead,
Christmas carols fly around the sky,
Making the positivity go high.

Christmas is my favourite time of the year,
Christmas trees, all so much I can't bear,
Please Santa, I don't want coal,
I've been good after all,
Milk and cookies are left for Santa,
All while me and my family sit and banter.

Adeena Siar (11)
Caterham High School, Clayhall

Diwali

The clear blue sky
The scent of flowers
The colours of Rangoli
And the sound of crackers

The gifts and sweets from dear ones,
And the getting of their love,
The light of the candles below,
And the dazzling fireworks up above.

Lighting lamps in our homes,
Making the less fortunate smile,
Pulling on new apparel,
Show our friends some style.

And paying respects to the god,
And decorating them for the thali,
This is what the occasion is all about.

Somya Bhootra (12)
Caterham High School, Clayhall

Christmas

It's Christmas Eve,
He's coming closer,
Everyone sleeping, tucked in tight.
The tree's up,
The lights are shining,
Mince pies, carrots and a glass of milk.
Soon enough they'll all be gone,
His bells are ringing.
Every house one by one,
Each get their gifts,
Surprises under the tree!

Dora-Rose Murtiera
Caterham High School, Clayhall

Santa

S anta will come out tonight
A nd deliver presents
N ear the
T ime of midnight
A nd the words you will hear... "Ho, ho, ho!"

George Burton (12)
Caterham High School, Clayhall

Snow

S nuggling up by the fire
N ight comes earlier every day
O pen the window to escape the foggy horizon
W inter has finally arrived!

Irum Jahan
Caterham High School, Clayhall

The Cold Is Here

The cold is here,
The sniffles have begun,
The double layers are needed.
The cold is making us blue,
But, the festive fun is arriving,
Trees and lights are up.
Ornaments are on the tree,
Christmas songs are on the TV,
Singing and dancing,
Holding hands and singing carols.
It's nearly time,
For the big day,
Everyone excited,
The elves are making mischief.
Every day, advent calendars are being opened,
Every day, it's getting closer,
And closer.
Until,
Today was the day,
It was Jesus's birthday.
Opening presents,

And opening cards,
Today's the day.
Of festive fun!
The day's over
The festive fun is fading away.
We'll hope to see it again next year!

Katelyn Huggins (10)
Cromer Junior School, Cromer

Elves

In a few days
Christmas will begin
Boys and girls
Cheer but...
The elves have come
They are everywhere
They may even have a sweet name
But don't think that's it
Because trust me it's not
They will eat your cookies
Open your calendar
Have your hot chocolate
Or even make a mess
Don't trust your elves
They are here, there and...
Everywhere.

Maisy Medler-Lake (10)
Cromer Junior School, Cromer

Mini Olympians

Animals who skate
Quick, let's look
Go and get the bait
And see them in action
We'll be the main attraction

Oh, please don't wobble
If you fall off
You'll have to hobble
I'll see you Mr Penguin
In the race, I hope you'll win.

Blossom Royall (9)
Cromer Junior School, Cromer

Winter Chanterelles

Meandering through a maze of snow-capped
trees and leaves
I stop to consider what is beneath my feet.
I can glimpse the vivid violet of a frosty webcap
And I know that its mycelium is secretly growing,
And growing,
And growing.
Hark! It is as if I can hear it whispering to me
To make me aware of its presence beneath the
snow surreptitiously.
Fungi!
These natural unnatural life forms are so weird
and wonderful:
Not a plant.
Not an animal.
But in between.
I tear my gaze away from the violet webcap
To look at the pale blue cloudless sky,
Where snowflakes are slowly fluttering to
the ground.
The air is so cool and pure

Free of the fumes and smoke
That you would find in London's slushy streets.
The wintry woods are my paradise
With the spiky brown branches of gnarled brown trees
And the trills, tweets and chirps of robins high up in them.
Together, they are the orchestra of the woods,
Which is sweeter than sugar
And more melodic than Beethoven's Für Elise.
I can smell the earthy, savoury aroma of the honeycomb-shaped morels,
The fruity scent of the chanterelle
And the mushroomy odour of the lilac-stemmed blewit
When I venture into the woods.
I can hear the rustling of frozen leaves in the whistling winter wind
When I venture into the woods.
I can see
The trees swaying as if greeting me,

The deep ocean-blue indigo milkcap rimmed with verglas
And the crimson colour of Frost's boletes
When I venture into the woods.
I can feel
The slimy waxcaps showing their marvellous scarlet colouring
The rough bark of ancient, majestic trees shrouded in icy crystals
And the bumpy milk-white spots on the bright red cap of the fly agaric
When I venture into the woods.
I can hear
The concert the birds are composing for the dazzlingly white snowdrops
When I venture into the woods.
I would rather be surrounded by this glacial beauty
Than become a billionaire
Or live in a palace.
The feeling of being carefree, joyful and excited,
Which can only be given to me by the woods,
Is worth more to me than silver and opals.
The moments I spend in the woods

Must be harvested like winter chanterelles
And savoured while they are fresh in my memory.

Sebastian Shelton (12)
Davenies School, Beaconsfield

The Winter Carnival

The winter carnival is like no other
All around you see light and colour
The smell of popcorn mixed with the winter breeze
But all of a sudden, it starts to freeze

The rides are super fast
Which one to go on first, which one to save for last

The rides with the loops
Will make you dizzy
The ladies with the hoops
Will make you tizzy

After the shows, the crowd gets wild
This place is divine and magical

Welcome to The Winter Carnival.

Alisha Bhandari (10)
Donibristle Primary School, Dalgety Bay

Winter's Night

W ind blowing through the trees,
I cicles hanging from the ledge,
N oises coming from the forest,
T rees blowing in the wind,
E verything is quiet,
R aindrops turn to ice,
'S now is falling softly.

N ever has it been so still,
I ce forming on the windows,
G littering stars in the night sky,
H ouses with warm fires all around,
T he day is almost here.

Chloe Diamond-Searle (10)
Donibristle Primary School, Dalgety Bay

The Ice Fox

One night I was on a stroll
When I saw a polar bear roll

Foxes like to run
You see them leaping and having fun

They have white fur
But they don't purr

They blend in the snow
Their cover is low

Ice foxes play
Then they have a great day

They are really nice
And love some ice.

Lotte Harry (10)
Donibristle Primary School, Dalgety Bay

Christmas Feelings

C hristmas
H appy
R eindeer
I cicles
S leigh
T urkeys
M erry
A nxious
S anta.

Millie Robertson (11)
Donibristle Primary School, Dalgety Bay

Snow Days

S now is falling all around
N ow let's go and have some fun
O utside we go
W anting to play in the snow.

Chloe D
Donibristle Primary School, Dalgety Bay

Merry Christmas

The clock struck eight,
As the kids ate.
They were excited to see what they got.
They went to the tree.
Wow, there was a lot!

As Mariah Carey sang,
The kids said, "Oh, dang!"
As they went out in the snow
They had to give their hands a good blow.

Santa still travelled across the world,
His sleigh did a little twirl.
The elves arrived back home.
They all roamed to the new gnome.

The kids ate a Christmas dinner.
Rudolph played reindeer games
To find out who was the winner.
The sound went from low to high.
The ground rumbled as they pounced around.

Riley Lamb (11)
Drapers' Academy, Romford

Countdown To Christmas

On the 1st day of December,
Santa gave to me, some songs by Mariah Carey.
On the 2nd day of December,
Santa gave to me, a chance to watch I'm
a Celebrity.
On the 3rd day of December,
Santa gave to me, a hot chocolate and a
warm cookie.
On the 4th day of December,
Santa gave to me, a cold, snowy morning.
On the 5th day of December,
Santa gave to me, a green, fluffy Christmas tree.
On the 6th day of December,
Santa gave to me, Last Christmas on the TV.
On the 7th day of December,
Santa gave to me, snowflakes falling on the street.
On the 8th day of December,
Santa gave to me, gingerbread men for me to eat.
On the 9th day of December,
Santa gave to me, snowmen in the frosty breeze.

On the 10th day of December,
Santa gave to me, a party with my family.
On the 11th day of December,
Santa gave to me, an opportunity to donate
to charity.
On the 12th day of December,
Santa gave to me, Sam Thompson winning I'm
a Celebrity.
On the 13th day of December,
Santa gave to me, The Grinch on the BBC.
On the 14th day of December,
Santa gave to me, a chance to open cards with
my family.
On the 15th day of December,
Santa gave to me, red and white candy canes.
On the 16th day of December,
Santa gave to me, a meet and greet in the grotto.
On the 17th day of December,
Santa gave to me, a visit with my grandparents.
On the 18th day of December,
Santa gave to me, exactly a week until
Christmas Day.

On the 19th day of December,
Santa gave to me, two Greggs mince pies.
On the 20th day of December,
Santa gave to me, six inches of fresh snow.
On the 21st day of December,
Santa gave to me, no more school until January.
On the 22nd day of December,
Santa gave to me, a binge-watch of
Christmas movies.
On the 23rd day of December,
Santa gave to me, a snowy Christmas lay-in.
On the 24th day of December,
Santa gave to me, Christmas Eve traditions.
On the 25th day of December,
Santa gave to me, my favourite Christmas.

Katie Cooksey (12)
Drapers' Academy, Romford

What Are You Doing This Christmas?

What are you doing this Christmas?
Perhaps putting on a new Christmas show?
Christmas shall be so fabulous!
Or may you kiss your wife under the mistletoe?

What shall you do this Christmas?
Should you go and play in the snow?
Don't forget your calendar!
Even though the wind may blow!

What may you do this Christmas?
Maybe stay up to see Rudolph's nose glow?
Put on some Christmas songs.
You may even hear the iconic, "Ho! Ho! Ho!"

Have a great Christmas, everyone.

Albert Penson (11)
Drapers' Academy, Romford

Winter Wonderland

Wrapping paper flying,
As they tear it off the walls,
The smell of cookies,
Gingerbread and pie
Mistletoe hanging.

Love is in the sky 'tis the season to be jolly,
Fa la la la la, lights are twinkling.
Snowflakes falling,
So much to see,

Ah, gather round the fire,
Sip some hot cocoa,
Sing Christmas carols,
Feeling oh so loco, the tree is sparkling,

Presents underneath,
Excitement in the air,
Can't contain my feet thinking 'bout the birth
of Jesus,
The reason for the season of love, hope, and joy,
gives us all a reason.

It's Christmas time, let's spread some love and peace on Earth,
From the stars above gather with family,
Make some memories this special day,
Means so much to me.

Decorations everywhere,
Red and green galore, Santa's on his sleigh,
Flying from door to door, children's laughter,
Echoing through the halls.

But let's not forget,
Those who have no home,
Let's spread some kindness,
So they're not alone.

Steven Davenport (14)
Drapers' Academy, Romford

A Christmas Winter Poem

Roses are red,
Violets are blue and purple,
Only in summer,
But now it's winter,
Brrr! It's cold,
Have hot chocolate
With marshmallows and some whipped cream,
All wrapped up just like a burrito...
Nice and cosy with family

Watch a movie or listen to Mariah Carey.
Others putting up their Christmas tree,
While your neighbours drink a cup of tea,
"Hehehe!" and "Hahaha!" are all you can
hear outside,
The snow is falling... down, down, down and down
Ding-Dong. Ding-Dong.
There are carollers waiting at the door to sing
to you
"Honey, go get the money!"
Down thy neighbours' presents are shared,

In the town hall, most of them are women,
A Christmas tree awaits everyone for its grand opening,
Five... four... three... two... one... wow!

Joy is the only thing you hear during this time of year,
It comes so slowly but when it arrives it goes so fast.

Alessya Birlea (12)

Drapers' Academy, Romford

One Starry Night

One starry night
It looks so bright
Look at the snow
And watch the stars glow.

Santa flies through on his sleigh
Hopefully lights up everyone's day
Santa's little helpers are busy
Sometimes they end up getting dizzy.

Rudolph and his reindeer
Have a lot of fears
Christmas Eve is near
And everyone's writing cards beginning with 'Dear'.

Everyone's having fun in the snow
While singing, "Let it snow, let it snow, let it snow"
Lay out your mince pies
But make sure Santa can still do up his flies!

Everyone's too excited to sleep
They're all dancing on their jingly feet

Santa is on his way
In his big, red sleigh.

Rudolph's nose is so bright
It brightens up the starry night
All the presents in his sack
They're all ready to be unpacked.

Aimee Doidge (12)
Drapers' Academy, Romford

Christmas Day

Every year on Christmas Day,
All the people run different ways.
Some people don't celebrate this time,
Some people celebrate and dine.

I look out to the snow,
But all I see is the winter glow.
By the sleigh,
All the reindeer wait to play.

As we wait for our gifts,
Santa lifts,
The wind blows,
As people kiss under the mistletoe

It's always cold,
It has been since the story was told.
As the stars appear in the sky,
Christmas Day says, "Bye-bye."

Ruby Teeder-Holland (14)
Drapers' Academy, Romford

Winter

Snow is falling all of outside,
Lay out Santa's mince pie,
And milk with pride.
Don't forget the carrot for the reindeer
Gotta love the season of Christmas cheer!
As trees and gardens get covered with snow,
Proudly kiss your wife under the mistletoe,
Wake up to chocolate 24 days in a row,
Whenever you're awake Santa will know!
Let it snow, let it snow
And watch the stars brightly glow.
Every Christmas, a kid would gradually grow,
And even the beliefs of Santa unfortunately let go.

Riley Ayres (13)
Drapers' Academy, Romford

A Winter Wonderland

W hile singing, 'Let It Snow!'
I t looks so bright
N orth Pole
T ree
E lves
R udolph

W hile it is snowing
O ne starry night
N o one is awake
D ancing around the living room
E verybody is having fun in the snow
R udolph and his red nose
L ay out your mince pie
A nd get lots of sleep
N orth Pole is looking good
D oing up the Christmas Tree.

Genevieve Eyoulou (12)
Drapers' Academy, Romford

The Magic Of Christmas

Snow, on a Christmas Eve night,
Starts shining ever-so bright.
Santa, on his red sleigh,
Led by the magic of Christmas.

A day, full of giving,
A dream come true to make it worth living.
Have fun with family, friends and more,
Led by the magic of Christmas.

One day, when everybody comes together,
Where families come to love, forever and ever.
So, be grateful for the magic of Christmas Eve
And make sure to put up a tree!

Harry Maskell (11)
Drapers' Academy, Romford

The Swinging Poem

The snow falling
My hope rises like the sun from the east.
My sister is jumping around like a flea.

Happiness is the glance I can see,
Salt pranks that are saltier than the sea.
I'm happy for the New Year.
It's good to see cheer.
Naughty children have fear.
Jolly Old Nick better hear.

Nothing like a warm chimney.
Oh, look at the Christmas tree!
Beautiful birds always feel free.
The best part is the feast!

Mirparham Ojaghihagh (12)
Drapers' Academy, Romford

Christmas Time

Christmas year,
Christmas time,
Christmas coming closer all the time,
Being kind,
Being there for family,
Feels very nice.

Joy here and joy there,
Joy is coming everywhere.
Presents here and presents there.
Presents everywhere,
Have a wonderful New Year and Christmas
Get cosy near the fire having warm hot chocolate
And remember to stay calm when Santa comes
to give your presents.

Andreja Buckovaite (11)
Drapers' Academy, Romford

Christmas

Christmas, it's Christmas!
Santa is just a little bit of magic away.
Snow covers every house and path with
Christmas cheer.
Cheer all around,
Gift-giving as a Christmas treat.
The weather has us in a jolly spirit.
Everyone's around with Christmas equipment out,
A turkey or two,
At their Christmas dinner.
Just a hop, skip and a jumping spirit away,
From being the best Christmas of all.

Tommy Cressey (13)
Drapers' Academy, Romford

Christmas Joy!

Christmas, where have you been?
You have the joy to bring
To share happiness and tears.
As I sit by the fire,
Drinking hot chocolate made from a pot,
Thinking how you will deliver Christmas
Without your helpers.
Santa, oh Santa, please help,
Give me joy,
Help Christmas bring its magic back up.
Santa, oh Santa, please come today,
As Christmas is never the same without
The joy you bring.

Keira Rumble (12)
Drapers' Academy, Romford

The Magic Of Christmas

St. Nicholas on his sleigh
Ready for the big day.
No messing around
He's already in his gown.

Elves finishing the making of gifts
Using the handy lifts.
Others decorate the Christmas tree
Filled with lots of glee.

Reindeer ready to take off into the sky
About to say goodbye.
Magic fills the air because this Christmas Day
Will be joyful in every way.

Harry Tate (14)
Drapers' Academy, Romford

Everyone Knows When It Starts To Snow

Everyone knows when it snows,
When the breeze cools and the wind blows.
When the air turns still and cold,
And the ever-lasting stories that are told.

When all the children come out to play,
And they get out their dusty sleigh,
And when the snow commemorates the start of the season,
And it defies all known logic and reason.

Everyone knows when it starts to snow.

Adiv Sharma (13)
Drapers' Academy, Romford

Winter Day

On a cold winter day
There are kids who play
Who still believe in Santa's sleigh.

On the winter trail
The inmates wail
Because they're spending Christmas in jail.
A reason could be treason
But it doesn't matter because of the season.

The children make snowballs
Which they throw at walls.
The snow is wet
Like the day we met.

Archie Baker (13)
Drapers' Academy, Romford

Christmas Night

The clock struck twelve,
Which woke up the elves,
Christmas Night began
Santa does it again!

Load up the sleigh,
No time to play.
Snow covered the ground.
No one was around.

Bells jingled.
Elves mingled.
The last house was found.

The night was over.
It was such a bother.
Merry Christmas to all!

Archie Best (11)
Drapers' Academy, Romford

Snow

I like snow.
I like it a lot.
I like building snowmen.
I haven't got a lot.
Snow, I don't have.
The snow is now melting
As the day goes on.
The snow has all melted.
I go inside
Away from the coldness
Put on my pyjamas
And have a hot chocolate.

Lily Grange (12)
Drapers' Academy, Romford

My Wish

A snowy night,
At a snowy sight.
The mood is bright
And the time is right.

Santa is in flight
And our smile is bright.
Waiting for our presents
That will arrive at midnight.

Joe Lambert (12)
Drapers' Academy, Romford

Glad

In this season,
There is no reason,
To be sad,
You should be glad.

I play in the snow,
While the stars glow.
I put gingerbread men in the oven,
There were over a dozen.

Isabelle Curtis-Rich (13)
Drapers' Academy, Romford

Ice Skating

I take a step
With my skates.
I slide onto the ice.
The world swirled
And I twirled
All around the winter sky.
I felt the breeze through my hair.
Christmas joy is everywhere!

Daria Scutaru (12)
Drapers' Academy, Romford

Through The Eyes Of A Hedgehog

I look out and see trees,
Dull with light from the moon.
I see glowing stars in the sky,
Small in the distance.
I see towering plants all around,
Droplets on every leaf.
As I go sit nestled in my hiding place,
Full of warm, cosy leaves,
Cold air wooshes past.
I snug deeper and deeper,
In a long, calming sleep.

Sophie W (12)
Framingham Earl High School, Framingham Earl

Festive Spirit

W hen Christmas was here, it was festive and great
I cy and cold, Grimsby was frozen over.
N ow Christmas is gone, and everyone is bored.
T hough it's a new year, we're still waiting for snow.
E ating the roast dinner was a blast.
R unning to your presents fast

W hy isn't the new year as exciting?
O ur friends and family were thrilled.
N ow it's actually here
D oesn't it make you miss last year?
E nd of the last and the start of a new
R eady to
L ive, laugh, love festive spirit
A fter it's done
N othing is fun
D one with the festive spirit till next year.

Oliver Newton (13)
Havelock Academy, Grimsby

Winter In Flanders

In the bleak mid-winter
Staring down a gun
My eyes are tired, my hands are cold,
In the morning sun

Do I have to shoot the Jerries?
Right between the eyes
Major Truss and Colonel Ben
Spinning us their lies

The whistles all fall silent,
As Christmas Day arrives
We drop our guns and raise our heads
Today will save our lives

Jerry is a father
He's got a wife and a son
Tomorrow I'll try to kill him
And he'll shoot me until the day is done

Now back to Smallheath and the Garrison.

Max Holness (15)
Havelock Academy, Grimsby

Winter Fun

Winter is the time for fun and cheer
Wishing for snow to play out during the day
Sitting by the fire to keep warm
Getting cuddled in bed or on the sofa
Ready for hot cocoa and a fun winter night

When it snows that's when the real fun begins

Sliding on ice
Making snow angels and snowmen
Laughing and smiling with your friends
Having real winter wonderland fun.

Jasmin Gordon (13)
Havelock Academy, Grimsby

Christmas Eve

Tossing and turning, struggling to sleep
Too excited for Christmas day
Snow falling and coating the ground
Ready for the children to build snowmen
Wondering what gifts, they'll get the next day
Christmas Day comes at last
Bells ringing, children screaming
Bags full of wrapping paper
The scent of Christmas dinner lingers
Through the cold morning air.

Ava Candy (12)
Havelock Academy, Grimsby

Snowy Christmas

Waking up on Christmas morning,
All the presents under the Christmas tree,
Don't be a Grinch, be jolly on Christmas,
You go outside and see the snow falling,
It's a Christmas miracle
Be in the Christmas spirit
Give and take
Make Christmas magical
Merry Christmas everyone!

Harry Ryley (13)
Havelock Academy, Grimsby

Winter

W arm and windy
I ce and snow
N ights wrapped up in blankets
T rees and lights
E lves and gifts
R eindeer and sleighs.

Jaya Gregson (13)
Havelock Academy, Grimsby

Christmas Spirit

The bright white moon
Lighting up the night
The icy road will make you trip and slip
Children playing without despair
As the Christmas spirit is in the air.

Charlie Blain (13)
Havelock Academy, Grimsby

Enchanting Wonders Of Winter Wonderland

The snowflakes twirl and swirl about,
Blanketing the earth in white.
A magical winter wonderland,
A sight so breathtakingly bright.

The air is crisp and cold,
With a wintery chill in the breeze.
The trees are dusted in white,
As if they were dipped in seas.

The snowflakes form a blanket,
Soft and delicate and pure.
It's a sight so beautiful,
It's like a dream come true.

The snowflakes look like diamonds,
Twinkling in the night sky.
A winter wonderland so enchanting,
It's a magical sight to see.

The snowflakes twirl and swirl about,
Bringing a wintery delight.
A winter wonderland of enchantment,
It's a beautiful wintery sight.

Michelle Evboifo (11)
International Community School London, Paddington

The Snowy Winter's Eve On The White Day

In winter's gentle grasp, a hush descends,
A world adorned in frost, where beauty blends.
Each flake, a tale of nature's artistry,
In silent dance, a winter symphony.

The trees stand tall, their branches dressed
in white,
A canvas painted by the pale moonlight.
The air is crisp, a whispered, chilly song,
As shadows play, the night is hushed and long.

Upon the ground, a blanket, pure and deep,
Where secrets of the season softly sleep.
Footprints mark a transient, fleeting trace,
As winter wraps the world in a cold embrace.

The hearth's warm glow invites with open arms,
A refuge from the biting winter charms.
Fireside tales, like embers, brightly burn,
Igniting hope as frosty tendrils turn.

A cardinal's crimson against the snow,
A burst of life when all seems hushed and slow.
Nature's resilient spirit is on display,
In winter's grip, a vibrant, fleeting day.

So, let us cherish winter's quiet grace,
Embrace the cold and let our spirits trace,
The beauty found in every snowy scene,
For in the frost, a world of dreams convenes.

Freddie Pritchard (12)
Llanishen High School, Llanishen

Christmas Day

It was Christmas Eve
We were setting up and decorating our tree
Hearing bells ringing through the night
Excited and overwhelmed
I couldn't wait, I was in a fright
Roaming my room, slowly falling asleep
Walking around, trying not to make a peep
I heard footsteps making a loud stomp
I heard someone eating, eating in chomps
I finally closed my eyes, falling asleep
I woke up later, excited to soon see my stocking
My tree was full of joy and happiness
Under the mistletoe, giving kisses
Seeing all the presents left me in shock
Giving and getting's the best part
We surrounded each other cutting the turkey
Smiling in joy as we dance having a
Christmas party
That’s the end of my poem I hope you enjoy

Have a very merry Christmas
And celebrate the birth of the baby boy.

Lilly Brayley (12)
Llanishen High School, Llanishen

Cold Christmas

W inter breeze, frosty and bright, is just such a delight.
I ce taking over the cold lonely neighbourhood.
N aughty children begging for forgiveness from Santa and his elves.
T all brave reindeer taking off for flight.
E veryone gathered around, celebrating the beginning of the new year.
R ight, what a great sight.

Amelie Langman (12) & Seren
Llanishen High School, Llanishen

Christmas Cheer!

Cuddly, warm, fuzzy and bright,
Drinking all the hot chocolate in sight!
Sharing snowglobes, admiring their beauty,
While we eat dinner as a family of foodies!

Building snowmen in the icy snow,
With people festively hugging under the mistletoe!
Settling down all warm and snug,
Not a creature stirring, not even a bug!

All is quiet,
All is calm,
It's time to celebrate Christmas!

Spread some joy,
Spread some love,
And most of all, don't be a grudge
Spread some Christmas cheer!

Enya O'Rourke (12)
Maesteg Comprehensive School, Maesteg

A Cold Winter's Night

Bells jingle,
The wind blows and snowflakes fall.
It is Christmas Eve night,
All asleep in joy and excitement.
In just a few hours, Santa Claus would be there!
Carrots, cookies, and milk await.
Christmas trees wait with no presents underneath,
Stockings empty.
A thud on the roof,
Steps come from above,
A thud in the chimney
Little Lilly knew who it was.
She went out of her room and walked down
the hallway.
Creakity-creak as she went down the stairs.
There he was, Santa Claus!
Munching on cookies,
Slurping on milk,
And stashing carrots in his coat.
Little Lilly ran upstairs
And snuck a camera to take her proof.

She ran downstairs all happy and proud.
She came downstairs to see he was gone!
An empty plate and glass,
A full stocking.
And the tree packed with presents.
And the Christmas spirit started to grow.

It's Christmas Day once again!
Streets empty
But filled with Christmas spirit once again.
Hot chocolate slurped,
Bellies full,
And presents unwrapped.
Spirit is high,
Everyone at home
No work
No shopping
No school
It's a holiday!
The only thing running is Christmas.

Tileah Summer (12)
Maesteg Comprehensive School, Maesteg

Winter

They say 'Merry Christmas' in the UK and America
They say 'Feliz Navidad' in Spanish
They say 'Joyeux Noel' in French
No matter where you're from it's still Christmas
Whether it's a stocking full of gold
Or a plain old lump of coal
It's still nice to know you were remembered
A decorated tree or a drowsy stump
Then there'll be presents when Santa comes
The stories we hear
And we'll laugh and cheer
If it's a cosy movie night by the fire
Or even just dinner with your family
If you're having a good time that's all that matters
Smile on your face and that look in your eye
People know it's Christmas
"What about New Year?"
Fireworks and a glass of wine
Someone to kiss when they drop the ball
We sing and dance
And drink too much and try not to fall

"What about the animals?"
Deep in sleep or even deeper
Some go hunting and some just 'chill'
Some are used to it
Some are not
"What about the weather?"
Snow keeps falling and icicles freeze
The trees are bare
The moon full by four o'clock
The wind is so cold,
Can you feel the breeze?
This winter
Whether you're gathered by the fire with hot chocolate
Or can hardly wait to open your presents
Snow or rain
Love or pain
It's still winter
Always the same
But never lame
It's still winter.

Brooke Till
Northview House School, Kilbarchan

Winter Wonderland

It was snowing like cats and dogs,
I walked out feeling like it was a special day.
I saw icicles and I touched them,
They were sharp like a blade.

On the very top of a little tree
There was a baby robin,
He was so cute and cuddly
And my brain had an idea...
So I walked on the crunchy snow
Picked up the soft, fluffy snow
And started building a snowman.
Then after I finished,
A weird snowball came out of nowhere
And then the snowballs went faster,
Hurling like meters, there were multiples!

Then I ran as fast as I could
Back to my house like a cheetah
Then I managed to flee and made it inside,
But finally, I'm inside.

I was cold like an ice cube,
I turned on the heater
And I was warmer now.
I went to the kitchen and got some milk
And made a chocolate cocoa
I turned on the fireplace
And chilled out on the couch,
I chilled like a bear.

Kamron Gibson (13)
Oak Wood Secondary School, Nuneaton

Winter

Out in the snow, coat and scarf.
I fell over, it gave me quite a mark.
Time to make the decision of my life.
Do I slip and fall or go inside?
Do I prefer the hot and calm
Or outside cold and fall?
Look at those icicles glisten and glow.
Now I've got to go, go, go.
I went inside nice and warm,
To drink some cocoa.
I went back outside with a little spin.
Looking at some roses
Covered in snow, they are gorgeous.
My boots were full of snow rocks.
So, I went back inside.
I locked all my locks the door was shut.
I was down near the fire sipping cocoa.
I lifted my head and looked to the right
The snow was melting, aww shucks,
Well, goodnight, snow, see you quite soon.
Another day awaits us very soon.

Jack Treadwell (13)
Oak Wood Secondary School, Nuneaton

The Winter Woods

I went out in the winter woods for some fun.
The bears in a cave were in a deep, deep
winter sleep.
I tried my best to not make a peep.
The ice was as cold as I go,
Good thing I dressed as warm as toast.
The trees were as high as I can see.
As the owl flew right in front of me.
My friends and I played in the snow,
We had a snowball fight!
Oh no, no, no.
We went down a hill on a sleigh,
As we slowed, hip, hip hooray.
Then it was time to go home after all the fun
And get some hot chocolate
And some biscuits in my rumble tum.

Taylor Barker
Oak Wood Secondary School, Nuneaton

Christmas Eve

On a loud, snowy night,
There was a child in his bed,
Waiting for Santa to bring him his gift.
A gift, he must have a gift,
He just has to have
He tossed and turned,
He just couldn't sleep.
All went silent as the boy heard footsteps
Coming from his old wooden rooftop.
Could it be?
It's got to be...
Santa it has to be!

Tyla-Jack Packer
Oak Wood Secondary School, Nuneaton

Winter Poem

I can see snow
I can see icicles
I can see frozen webs
I can see frozen trees
I can see a snowman
I can see the wind
I can see birds, robins
I can see spiders
I wear a coat
I wear gloves
I wear a scarf
I wear a hat
I wear winter clothes because it is very cold.

Alexa Gibbs (13)
Oak Wood Secondary School, Nuneaton

Winter

The ice is very cold, not a place for the old.
They throw the snow and the birds will go.
Snow is fun.
The footsteps are big.
The spider's webs are icy.
The big snowman has twigs for arms
And a carrot for a nose.

Ryan Rollason Trevitt
Oak Wood Secondary School, Nuneaton

I Can See...

I can see the white fluffy snow.
I can see the sharp icy icicles.
I can see the half-broken snowman.
I can see the shining bright sun.
I can see the frosty icy cobweb.
I can see people having a snowball fight.

Oliver Read (13)
Oak Wood Secondary School, Nuneaton

Winter Poem

The icicles are sharper than a knife.
The snow is crunching when you walk on it
The spiderwebs shine in the light.
The snow looks like icing on the trees.
The water freezes,
It is shimmering in the sunlight.

Lucas Grace (13)
Oak Wood Secondary School, Nuneaton

Winter

The icicles look like icebergs
I like to make a snowman.
I like fun in the snow.
I wear a hat, a scarf, a coat and gloves
Because it is very cold.
The snowman has a carrot nose
And stones for his eyes.

Harriet Lenton (13)
Oak Wood Secondary School, Nuneaton

Snow

I love to throw massive snowballs
And make people run.
I like to wear my shorts
And they turn my legs blue!

Keegan Mitchell
Oak Wood Secondary School, Nuneaton

A True Winter

Winter is the time for comfort,
For good food and warmth,
A time to be remembered,
For blizzards and snowstorms.

We snuggle by the fire,
Watching the dancing flames,
A time to admire,
Eating minty candy canes

Christmas trees all decorated,
Carol singers prowling the streets,
Parents staying caffeinated,
Baby Jesus lying beneath his crib sheets

Stars watching down from heaven,
Children running home from their last lesson,
St Nick readying his sleigh,
Giving children gifts so they can play.

Theo Somers (11)
Sandringham School, St Albans

Christmas Goodies

Mince pies, oh so nice
A slice or a whole
Oh, the snow is so thick
Winter is so wild
And quick and cold
Some figgy pudding
Cooking Christmas cookies
Goodies with Christmas hoodies
And the figgy pudding still cooking.

China-Rose Smith (10)
Seadown School, Worthing

Christmas

Cold, chilly, bitter weather, hot cocoa in my cup.
The fireplace is lit, stockings are hung,
and the Christmas tree is up.
Presents wrapped like a treasure chest.

So much snow, get ready for a snowball fight.
Kids laughing and having fun
getting hit by snowballs.

The evenings are starting to get dark,
The Christmas tree was bright,
so bright it guided me home.
Kids saying, "Christmas is tomorrow!"
then off they went to bed
The next day stockings were filled
and presents opened, giving their family a hug
And having Christmas dinner.
This is the true meaning of Christmas.

Isabelle Mitchell (10)
St Bartholomew's CE Primary School, Stourport-On-Severn

Icicles

Glistening and shimmering from the sun.
They melt and drip down onto the floors.
They even melt in front of doors.
They appear all over hanging
upside down or the right way up.
Pups hit the icicles with their paws
hitting them to the floor for the fun of things.
They are just like little spikes
that can appear anywhere overnight.
Drip, drip, drip, splosh that's the sound of them
melting and breaking into a puddle.
As the kids shout, the icicles shatter and shake.
They shine in moonlight and sunlight.
They never stop shining for long.

Jessica Evans (11)
St Bartholomew's CE Primary School, Stourport-On-Severn

Christmas

Lustrous, delicate, shimmering, glittering baubles,
Hanging on the Christmas tree
Candy canes, stars, angels, tinsel,
LED lights, all scream Christmas to me!

Christmas Eve children wrapped up,
all snug in their beds,
And presents under the tree, no prayer left unsaid.

Children waking up ecstatic,
they run downstairs to see,
Their presents left by Santa,
memories for you and me.

Outside: *crunch, snap, crash*,
Children playing and having fun.
Snow, frost and lots of families
playing together in the winter sun.

Charlie Collins (10)
St Bartholomew's CE Primary School, Stourport-On-Severn

Christmas

Cold, breezy, icy snow crunching
As I walk through the snow.
Splish, splash.
Children jumping in puddles.
Children playing and having fun.
Children sticking out their tongues
To catch snowflakes in their mouth.
Snowballs flying back and forth in the air.
People wiping ice off their car windows.
People scoffing their mouths with
Christmas turkey.
Children's parents pray before dinner.
People filling their mouths.
Christmas pudding.
Kids playing with their new toys,
Giggling out loud.
Families coming together.

That is what Christmas means to me.

Alfie Collins (10)
St Bartholomew's CE Primary School, Stourport-On-Severn

Winter Wonderland

Gliding, falling, floating.
Snowballs are driving home for Christmas.
Lights are bright, extremely bright.
Guiding me home on the long winter's night.
Stockings filled with sweet treats
Santa rushed down the chimney.
Delicate baubles on the tree.
Christmas dinner for you and me.
Decorated snowmen and families playing
in the fresh snow.
Cold, extremely cold, freezing.
The sound of the blizzard going *swoosh, woosh!*
Presents wrapped under the tree,
Santa came through the door with his magical key.

Ava Wilkes (11)
St Bartholomew's CE Primary School, Stourport-On-Severn

Christmas

Angels calmly perched on the branches of a tree.
Watching over you and me.
Kids drifting to sleep, so quiet you can't hear
a peep.
Santa landing on the roof, reindeer plodding,
The *clip clop* of their hooves.
Endless memories of Christmas Day:
Elves eating all the candy canes,
Rudolph getting the biggest carrot,
Santa eating all the mince pies,
Snowflakes falling on the ground.
Santa wheezed off with a, "Ho! Ho! Ho!"
Merry Christmas and a happy new year.

Harry Furnival
St Bartholomew's CE Primary School, Stourport-On-Severn

Christmas

Calm and relaxing, icy and cold.
Driving home for Christmas, lights bright and bold.
Snowmen, wet feet, smiles and rosy red cheeks.

Decorations outside of the home,
Nobody should be alone.
The winter sun is as beautiful as ever.
People celebrate with families, together.

The snow glistens like glitter, memories embedding
Lots of presents, hot chocolates and sledging.
Cheerful children out in the snow.

Crunch! Crunch! Crunch!

Leo Braley (10)
St Bartholomew's CE Primary School, Stourport-On-Severn

Winter Wonderland

Cool, bitter, drenched.
Beautiful blizzards gliding through the Arctic.
Christmas trees shimmer like a diamond.
Stockings filling, full to the brim, overfilling!
Roast dinners being cooked
Potatoes, Yorkshire puddings, turkey,
all scrumptious.
It's a memorable Christmas.
Stockings being filled
Family time together,
This is Christmas.

Alexander Mattinson (11)
St Bartholomew's CE Primary School, Stourport-On-Severn

Winter

The season of joy
A blanket of snow as white as clouds every day
Christmas carols of a baby on hay
Decorated with lights and trees
With baubles, lights and popcorn on a string
Snowmen being built
Lights as bright as the night sky filled with stars
Whistle, whistle the blow of the flute
Winter: the season of joy computes.

Leona Warren (10)
St Bartholomew's CE Primary School, Stourport-On-Severn

Christmas

Christmas is two days away.
Usually, I'm excited for Christmas
But this year it's different
I don't feel like I'm in the Christmas mood
I feel like I've been failing myself
Like I've ruined who I worked to be
I eat my candy canes in bed
Deciding if I'm in the mood to wake up at 5am on Christmas Day
Like I usually do,
But this year is different
I'm not a child any more
Optimistic and energetic by Christmas Eve, Eve
Or too awake to go to sleep on Christmas Eve,
Excited about all the presents coming the next day
This year my presents vanished
They were there
Now they are not
"Is Saint Nick punishing me?"
My inner child
Asks my tired brain

Opening my presents makes me happy
It reminds me of the optimistic child I used to be
But someone took that away
Making me sadder than I already am
I'm going through something
Worse than before
In my favourite season
The time of my birthday and Christmas
All I can do is sit in silence, as we watch Christmas movies on the couch
And hope that Saint Nick will bring my presents back
So the person I used to be
Will come back too.

Aliyah Fraser
St Mark's West Essex Catholic School, Harlow

A Winter Trio

As the clock ticks towards the stroke of twelve,
Listen close, my friend, as stories swell.
The New Year's on the horizon, can't you see?
A fresh start beckoning for you and me.

Whispers of resolutions, promise in the air,
A chance to begin anew, to show we care.
"I'll chase my dreams," someone vows,
Another one, "I'll mend what's broken somehow."

Underneath the stars, we stand as one,
Welcoming. The New Year has just begun.
Raise a glass of the future yet unknown,
To the seeds of dreams that we have sown.

Here's to the journey, the twists and turns,
In the dialogue of time, as the New Year yearns.
Together, let's step into the unseen,
In this moment, a canvas is pristine.

Gather 'round let me spin a tale,
Of a Christmas night, where wishes set failed.

Snowflakes danced, oh, such a sight,
Covering the town in a blanket of white.

Lights adorned each tree with grace,
A symphony of colours fills every space.
Families huddled by the fireplace's gleam,
Sharing stories, in the Christmas dream.

Families gather by the hearth's warm glow,
A shared embrace, love to bestow.
Gifts exchanged, with hearts aglow,
In the season's spirit, friendships grow.

Gifts wrapped in ribbons, a festive array,
Exchanged with love on this special day.
Carols echoed, a familiar tune,
Underneath the glow of the December moon.
In this season's glow, let kindness reign,
A timeless message, peace of Earth to attain.
May your Christmas be merry, and your joy walk.

Step outside, feel the winter's breath,
A quiet conversation with nature's depth,

The air is crisp, the ground aglow,
In this winter tale, let the stories flow.

Trees stand bare, like storytellers tall,
Sharing the secrets of snow's soft fall.
Footprints mark the path we tread,
In this dialogue with winter, where tales
are spread.

Sunsets paint the sky in hues so bright,
A canvas of warmth in the cold night.
Nature whispers in the hush of snow,
A silent conversation, soft and slow.

By the fireplace, tales come alive,
Of snowy landscapes, where dreams revive.
Yet, in each frosty, quiet air,
A connection, a story we all share.

Rosie Ashall (14)
The Birley Academy, Sheffield

The Night Before Christmas

In the cold, the sky so high, nothing can really hide.
The snow beneath me seems to listen as I see it glisten.
The night, perhaps above me there is light.
Up above from afar, a twinkle and sprinkle from a star.
As I listen from afar, the twinkle and sprinkle rings
As though it's made more art.
I turn to see what once was green, a blanket now lay in it.
The night is so lonely yet so full of life.
Almost as though it wasn't right.
What a wondrous night.
But now, the night lights flicker so it's time to say goodnight.

Tahera Gmucova (12)
The Birley Academy, Sheffield

Frosty Land Of Enchantment

A stampede of snowflakes emerged out of the sky,
The wind roared without being shy.
An icy, warm, white blanket blinded the night,
The beauty was like no other time.

In the wintry, snowy land,
We will create a majestic snowman
And have a snowball fight
Till we are drained for the twilight.

Some staying inside,
Avoiding the frosty time.
Staying put next to the fireplace,
Gulping hot chocolate without a trace.

Winter is a time of year,
Where most look forward to cheer.
The sight of snowfall near,
Childhood days can be recalled here.

Icicles hang from rooftops without no fear,
Sparkling like jewels, crystal and clear.
Enjoy the season without disapproval,
And prove what joy this wonderland can bring.

Kabisha Manmatharajan (14)
The Birley Academy, Sheffield

Frostbite

The frostbite prepared to take over England.
As the Atlantic melted, England got colder
and colder.
The polar bears howled in pain as their houses
were being taken
Once again.
At this time in the UK, you would call it Christmas.
The magic arrived in England
But you could say hell week arrived in the Arctic.
The wind howled at the snow piled on top
of houses.
Frostbite prepared to take over England.

Jae Ejogbamu (12)
The Birley Academy, Sheffield

Winter... What A Beautiful Season

Delicate snowflakes, fall from the cold, beautiful steel-grey sky.
Dancing like the most elegant ballerina.
As the glimmering snow settles on the cold paving and the rooftops of the villages,
Families emerged from their cosy homes and made small snowmen
And appreciated the breathtaking view of the Aurora Borealis in the midnight sky.
What a beautiful season!

Lily-Mae Morton (13)
The Birley Academy, Sheffield

Winter

W hen the air becomes chilly
I nside, warm fires are lit
N ice hot cups of cocoa are brought out
T rees become bare but stand proud
E ven the hardest of snowfall can't separate people
R emember, enjoy your winter memories.

Ella Cree (12)
The Birley Academy, Sheffield

Winter

In the winter's grasp, a world transformed;
A blanket of snow, a delicate lace.
The branches were blanketed in a silver layer
of white,
Shrouded in an elegant lace of ice.

The ground, so white and frozen, the frost, so cold,
Makes way for a winter wonderland to unfold.
The air crackles with an icy touch,
As if a winter fairytale has spun a spell foreseen.

The home, a place of cosiness, a fire to ignite,
A warmth to chase away the chill of the night,
Inside, a winter fire roars, a warmth to hold,
A symbol of love and kindness that unfolds.

Winter, a season of hope's cheer;
A time for family and a time to hold dear,
A time to reflect, a time to breathe,
A season of light, a season to believe.

Amirah Adeniji (11)
The Sydney Russell School, Dagenham

Winter

Silvery snowflakes frolicking, each one unique, each one united;
As beacons of hope in a world of tragedy and misfortune
Enchanting trees with no falling leaves with subtle distortion
Timeless holiday shopping always blown out of proportion

Everyone's wrapped up warm in their best winter attire
Whilst they huddle up by the blazing fire
You can hear Christmas carols being sung by a comforting choir

The bitter wind gushes in your face
It refuses to give you any space
So you decide to embrace

Dark mornings, cold evenings galore
Reminiscing of the heatwave before
Slipping on ice and defrosting the car and all

You know that deep in your soul
Winter has a special role
Even if the chill in the air is like the North Pole

Wintertime is full of fond memories to make
Delicious treats to bake
Stunning sights to intake

Winter is a season we all indeed cherish
It truly makes our hearts flourish
So before it perishes

Have fun and laugh and play
Make the most out of each day
Before the festive season withers away...

Amy Rodriguez-Ahmed (12)
The Sydney Russell School, Dagenham

Winter

Feel icicles, towering over you like a sinister skyscraper
Feel the snow, dropping like emotions.
Not really knowing where it comes from, or how.
Feel snow catapulting, like someone's happiness, like someone's anguish

Feel winter, happy, relaxed, cold, ominous, baleful, eerie.
Hurry now, times have changed and people have changed.
The seasons have changed, from autumn to winter.
Get ready for an unendurable, agonizing winter.

Salma Abdulai (12)
The Sydney Russell School, Dagenham

Winter Snow

Oh snow, you're so white
You shine so bright in the night

When you fall and touch the ground
You make a beautiful twinkling sound

Oh snow, you're so cold
Or at least that is what I was told.

Daniya Nazim
The Sydney Russell School, Dagenham

I Hate Winter

I hate winter.
The snow goes in my boots.
My nose goes run, run, run,
And my ears get stuffed up too.

My body starts to freeze,
I might have a disease.
I think I'm going to sneeze.
It's because of this horrible breeze!

And here is some advice,
Just don't go on the ice.
Your footing's not precise,
You'll start spinning like a dice!

And that's why I hate winter.
The cold, the flu, the aches,
Sometimes I wish,
It could all just be erased!

Chloe Swain
Weldon Village Academy, Weldon

The Christmas Recipe

Firstly, take a pinch of Christmas Eve joy,
Then, bring the enticing aroma
of the turkey to the table.

Grab a chiselled blade, slice and add
in the turkey for everyone to feast,
Next, season with Christmas festivities
and traditions used for many years.

Now, combine jumping out of bed
and merrily unwrapping presents
lying below the tree to your bowl,
While mixing in an entertaining snowball fight
with everyone around.

When the mixture is cold to the bone,
combine sips of a steaming hot chocolate
warming you from the inside out,
Last but not least, relish
and enjoy the magic of Christmas.

Gezim H (11)
Wheatley CE Primary School, Wheatley

A Recipe For A Cosy Winter

First, gather your family and pets
for some festive fun,
Next, get ready to sprinkle in
some Christmas cheer for all to hear.

Now it's time to make
an enticing, irresistible pancake,
So collect your nearest and dearest,
ready for a Christmas movie.

Quickly, add in the patience of a saint
lasting until the morning,
Wait patiently for the mixture to glow,
while adding in some playful snow.

Carefully stir in the ingredients
for a delicious morning feast,
Taking drops of relaxation
for an afternoon soothing bath.

Waft in the aroma of the crisp turkey
sitting on the table,
And the treat of a gooey hot chocolate
overloaded with oozing marshmallows.

Imogen J (11)

Wheatley CE Primary School, Wheatley

Winter Fest

First, gather family and friends for festive cheer,
After that, season the cheer with a bit of laughter
and snow and you're ready to go.

Actually, you need the sparkles of the frosty grass
you need to split it half and half,
Specks off the cosy fire make the flames
go higher and higher,

Hot chocolate with marshmallows
and some cream and have a dream,
Icicles as sharp as knives just remember to thrive,
Chocolate melting in my mouth as bright as a light.

Cut up the turkey don't have jerky,
Now sprinkle that frosty grass
and you'll have a blast
And you're ready just be steady.

Kane F (11)
Wheatley CE Primary School, Wheatley

This Is My Christmas

First, gather family and friends
to get ready for the festive fun to begin,
Next, think of the gift you most desire.

Take a nap when you're done and focused,
Hope for mountains of presents
waiting for you beneath the Christmas tree.

Add the aroma of the freshly made chicken
tingling beneath your nose,
Sit around the table with endless joy and laughter
while pulling crackers.
Bang! Bang! Bang!

When your family is ready to eat,
be prepared for the feast of the year,
Be overwhelmed with your family
and friends by your side,
Have fun with the best Christmas ever.

Sol Smith (10)
Wheatley CE Primary School, Wheatley

One Snowy Night

From my cosy corner beside the window
I see a winter wonderland of crunchy snow!
I reach out and feel it, the first flake in the sky,
And I feel a small shiver of dancing delight.
The trees stretch out their arms,
all adorned with cold ice,
I feel happy and warm
and the weather almost feels nice.
But sadly, the snow's gone as quickly as it came,
The sun melted it all, but it feels no shame.
Feeling quite underwhelmed, I slunk to my bed.
With a million memories circling my head.
Perhaps come the morning it will snow once again.
I'll sleep, safe and warm, in my bed until then.

Bryony Hartnell Murphy (9)
Wheatley CE Primary School, Wheatley

Winter With Me

Firstly, add a sprinkle of frost for the beginning,
Secondly, gather some oysters
and a pinch of glitter.

Afterwards, throw in some random baubles,
Then, play Mexican Christmas music
all through the night.

Now, drop in some sweets,
chocolates and marshmallows,
Carefully, pour a pint of mulled wine.

Softly, bake a galette in January,
Merrily, take a trip to St. Nick's castle,
Peacefully, watch the sunrise above a silver lake.

Then in the evening, dance in the snow,
And adore your winter from the beginning
to the end of the season.

Agatha Q (10)
Wheatley CE Primary School, Wheatley

Max's Magical Winter Recipe

First, gather your nearest and dearest,
ready for a festive feast,
Then, add the enticing aroma of all things
Christmas fills the air around you,
Season with the laughs, cheers and infinite singing.
Sprinkle in kind like confetti to everyone around,
Next, pour in bright white snow
to glow the world around you,
Dust with steaming hot chocolate,
enticing everyone near,
Whilst shaking, feeling and smelling the gifts
lying under the Christmas tree,
Pines falling creating an ice rink beneath your feet,
Laughs, smiles and tears of joy
are seen and heard for miles.

Max A-H (11)
Wheatley CE Primary School, Wheatley

Recipe For A Winter Wonderland

First, gather five crunchy leaves
and make a snowball,
After that, gather your family and friends
and sprinkle a bit of festive cheer.

Sprinkle in...
Season cheer, laughter and singing
with a tad bit of joy.

Now get a hot coco and make sure to have
mini marshmallows next to a warm cosy fire.

Grab your mittens and your nice fluffy warm coat
and go outside.

Put your hand out and let the
white fluffy snow settle,
Watch the snow blanket the garden
and build a snowman.

And spread your little holiday and festive cheer.

Harry Wakefield (10)
Wheatley CE Primary School, Wheatley

Shaye's Winter Fest

Firstly, gather siblings and parents
ready for some festive fun,
Now mix in the sharpest icicles that can be found.

Sprinkle in some magic full of fun,
Now give it a stir and make it a bun.

Next, add some slime turning it the colour lime,
Add two raindrops of snow
to make the potion glow.

Take a handful of the best Christmas vibes,
Don't forget to add some water from the tides.

Then add the best presents for all,
Make sure everyone has a ball.

Finally, add some magical Christmas dust,
Having fun at this time is a must!

Shaye F (10)
Wheatley CE Primary School, Wheatley

Warming Winter Recipe

First, gather family and friends while
reaching for some Christmas fun,
Secondly, stir in your snuggly winter clothes.

Then take a trip to your favourite place
to gather some fluffy snow,
Now add in your perfect recipe for the best hot
chocolate, don't forget the melting marshmallows
and cream as white as snow.

Add a sprinkle of magical Christmas cheer,
Now the most important part!

Give it a stir and put all
your Christmas spirit into it,
Finally, sit down, snuggle up and wait patiently
while watching your favourite Christmas movie.

Carmen Powell (9)
Wheatley CE Primary School, Wheatley

Festive Fun!

First, grab your closest friends and family
for the ultimate festive fun,
Next, fluff up some snowballs and bombard
the family with tiny balls of snow!

Sprinkle in the decor, and Christmas fun for all,
And crush up frosted crunchy leaves
with a morning mist.

Start the roaring, blazing and crackling fire
and get cosy and comfortable,
Mix up the snacks and the tasty treats.

Then, give out thanks and cheer,
Receiving, giving and celebrating.

Glinting stars in a frosty, deep
and dark winter night completes your recipe.

Ryan S (11)
Wheatley CE Primary School, Wheatley

My Winter Recipe

First, fill your bowl with hot chocolate
and marshmallows
Next, the owl's hoots, when it snows.

Then, the red feathers from a fluffy robin's tummy,
After that, Brussels sprouts, all small and yummy.

Sprinkle with the crust of the bright light moon,
Add a dozen Christmas films, coming soon.

Season with the pink and purple morning sky,
Drop in the icy wind, letting the small birds fly.

Snuggle up close to friends,
loved ones and pets, too,
Now you'll have a bitterly cold winter,
all nice and new!

Caitlin P
Wheatley CE Primary School, Wheatley

Wonderful Winter Recipe

First, gather your nearest and dearest,
and make several snowballs,
After, throw them at each other,
and make the spirits jump around together.

Come inside and make a bubbly hot chocolate
and share it with your peers,
Watch the fire spit and crackle,
wrapped up warm in a comforting bubble.

After that go up to your loft and
collect your Christmas ornaments,
Carefully climb down the ladder
and put up your tree.

Decorate it with care, and place it on all with love.
Now have yourself a wonderful Christmas.

Delilah Cook (10)
Wheatley CE Primary School, Wheatley

The Frosty Fun

First, gather as many snowballs as possible,
Next, grab some warming gloves
to get ready to cause some chaos.

Sprinkle in some Christmas revenge
to everyone in sight,
Then, swirl into a cup of
your favourite Christmas treats.

Season with your favourite festive sprinkles,
Add a pinch of laughter, joy and cheer.

Whilst decorating in glittery frost
from the ground below,
Then, throw like you never have before.

Sprinkling festive fun to all involved,
Creating a frosty masterpiece for all nearby.

Evie D (11)
Wheatley CE Primary School, Wheatley

The Day Of Christmas

First, gather your family for a whole lot of fun,
Now, go for a walk in the winter snow.

Once you're back grab a heated Christmas dinner,
And eat it with the family together.

Now, open your presents one at a time,
Make sure you open them all and be kind.

The family is gathered around the room,
Smiles can be seen from ear to ear.

And now it's time for the snowball fight,
Who is going to win? Will it be a delight?

Now it's the end of the day,
It's time to lay your sleepy head.

Milo McSweeney (10)
Wheatley CE Primary School, Wheatley

Recipe For A Winter Wonderland!

First, gather a handful of Arctic, frosty and frozen
snowballs for a festive feast,
Next, add some Christmas tree magic
to brighten the day,

Sprinkle in some gooey marshmallows
to sweeten the treat,
Add a pinch of bitter-cold icicles,

Season with magical snowflakes
taken from all around,
Drop in some holly to make the recipe jolly,

Pour some sweet and delicious
hot chocolate into the mix,
Then, warm gently over a crackling fire,

Now your winter will sparkle
with white frosty snow!

Mia Ayres (11)
Wheatley CE Primary School, Wheatley

Winter's Magic

First, gather snuggly cosy warm clothes,
Secondly, gather all the best snow.

Then, sprinkle in warm hugs
for your family and friends.
Next, add the one and only hot chocolate
(including gooey marshmallows and cream).

After that, you will need Rudolph's
special Christmas shimmer,
Involving your favourite winter wonder memories!

Now it's time to stir in your favourite winter movie,
Sit back and wait patiently, the mixture will glow,

Enjoy by the crackling fire
for the best winter magic.

Leyla Bourne (9)
Wheatley CE Primary School, Wheatley

Winter Wonderland

Firstly, gather all your family and friends
for some festive fun.

After that, mix in all your wintery joy,
and decorations,
Adding a sparkle of magic to the mix.

Then collect some soft snowballs,
bolting through the air,
Sharp icicles everywhere.

Children laughing in the snow,
the morning mist lingers.

Frosty trees in the distance,
bent like twisted fingers.

So snuggle up this winter,
and live the best you can.

That is all you need for your wintery recipe...

Owen J (10)
Wheatley CE Primary School, Wheatley

Snow

Quickly, quietly, floating, falling,
As elegantly as a swan.
Falls to the ground
Soon to be found.
And people can have fun!

Icy ballerinas dancing swiftly
Through the air.
Coats the ground in fluffy mattresses
For people soon to be there.

Fluffy white snow on my fingertips,
Crisp and soft and cold,
Sharp twang of coldness.
Wiping it off fences, new and old.

Gentle, calm, bright,
Floating silently,
To the ground,
Landing with a bow.

Charlotte Walker (10)
Wheatley CE Primary School, Wheatley

The Christmas Feast

First, gather your family and friends to get ready
for a Christmas festive feast,
Next, get three snowballs
and start a snowball fight.

Then, go to the fire and have a cosy hot chocolate,
After, return to the snow
and make beautiful snow angels.

Then put some aroma of Christmas feeling,
Sprinkle with glowing glitter,
Get the turkey out of the boiling oven
and eat with your family.

Next, get in your cosy bed,
And sleep for the next day.

Andrei B (10)
Wheatley CE Primary School, Wheatley

The Night Before Wonder...

First, gather blankets and colourful pillows,
Mix in hot chocolate with sprinkles
and marshmallows.

Next, gather handfuls of snow-covered ice,
Put in your dreams and
make sure they're extra nice!

After, cosy up by the blazing fire,
Fall asleep listening to the beautiful choir.

Add mountains of presents to your potion,
And also lots of jolly emotions.

Finally, adding family and friends,
I hope your Christmas has an amazing end!

Celia Y
Wheatley CE Primary School, Wheatley

A Perfect Winter's Recipe

First, gather some of your closest family
and friends, and get ready for festive fun.

Then, pour in some hot chocolate,
cream, and marshmallows,
Sprinkle with presents, endless wrapping,
and enjoyment for all.

Then listen to laughter from your
nearest and dearest,
Get cosy next to the roaring fire,
And watch a comforting Christmas film.

Though the rain will fall,
Though the wind will blow,
Your winter will glitter with joyful snow.

Lily W (10)
Wheatley CE Primary School, Wheatley

A Winter's Recipe

First, grab a handful of snowflakes
with the fluffiest mittens you can find,
Next, find a collection of crunchy,
frosty leaves and drop them in with care.

Sprinkle a fair amount of the soft, fluffy snow
and stir your pot until it all starts to glow,
Season with the glinting ice from below,
your numb body will tingle with joy.

Then, warm it up with a drop of hot chocolate
and gooey mini marshmallows,
Now sit down and enjoy your warming winter glow!

Elsie Morris (9)
Wheatley CE Primary School, Wheatley

Festive Feels

Firstly gather your family and friends
for some festive fun,
After that, you will need three snowballs,
with a sprinkle of festive sugar and holiday cheer.
You need your mittens and scarf
to wrap around the snowman's cheer,
Add some buttons and a crunchy carrot
to make it hear.
Come inside for some bubbly hot chocolate,
covered with warm hugs and love.
Wrap up warm in front of the crackling fire,
Put your feet up as it's nice and quiet.

Rosie W (10)
Wheatley CE Primary School, Wheatley

A Wonderful Winter Wonderland

When you want some winter wonderland,
First, gather family and friends.

Second, cosy up by the roaring fire,
Next, find a fantastic feast.

After that, bundle up neat and nice,
Then, crush icicles as long as limbs.

Once that's done, unwrap a pile of presents,
Making hot chocolate with gooey marshmallows.

Play with cousins, hiding, running and frolicking,
Sprinkle some snow
and wait for another winter wonderland.

Bobby R (11)
Wheatley CE Primary School, Wheatley

Magical Recipe For Winter!

First, gather some hot cocoa in a mug,
Then, mix in some toasted fluffy marshmallows.

With a sprinkle, add a little bit of joy,
Add a pinch of your favourite sweets and treats.

Now grab a cosy, fuzzy and fluffy blanket
so you won't get too chilly,
Now for the amazing part!

Snuggle up with friends and family
Though trees will stand bare,
though winds bluster and blow
Now your winter will glitter with sparkling snow.

Ella P (10)
Wheatley CE Primary School, Wheatley

Wintertime

Gliding, silkily and sparkly,
Snow falling away,
As cold as ice,
For me no one to play with,
Snowflakes twinkling like stars,
People are frozen to the bone,
Smoke fuming from chimneys,
As I am all alone.
Laying snow on roofs like bed sheets,
People rushing to a fun fair,
Crack! ice as people slip,
As I am cuddling my teddy bear,
Each gentle star lit up by moonlight,
Like an unreal painting.

Gabby Jones (10)
Wheatley CE Primary School, Wheatley

The Recipe For Christmas Chaos!

First, gather your nearest and dearest
ready for a fabulous feast,
Secondly, add in your siblings or stepmothers
along with some spectacular spice.

Thirdly, stir in the sparkling streets
and breathe in the ice-cold breeze,
Next, season with a dozen frozen acorns
creating a nutty mix.

Swirl into your mix with a bit of a winter's bisque,
Finally, decorate with a sprig and a twig or two.

Livia C (11)
Wheatley CE Primary School, Wheatley

Frost

Calmly, gracefully, floating, gliding,
Jumping from lamp light to lamp light,
Icy dancers twirling through the sky,
Performing, frozen, forming routines,
I feel them nipping on my cold pink nose;
my hands feel a touch of ice,
The dancers tiptoed across the blanket of snow
under some dappled sunlight like mini spotlights,
Bowing, fluttering, beautifully,
on the soft winter icing.

Rose (9)
Wheatley CE Primary School, Wheatley

A Special Winter Wonderland

Firstly gather friends to make a fire,
Then have a festive feast.

Sprinkle snow on a snowman's head,
And put in a carrot for a nose,
Add two twigs for its arms.

Decorate the tree with tinsel and lights,
Make a hot chocolate to warm up.

Look out of the window with a sight of joy,
Put on layers to wrap up warm,
Wake up tomorrow for a cold school day.

Nixon A (11)
Wheatley CE Primary School, Wheatley

Snow

Twinkling, shimmering, glistening, majestic.
Twinkling as bright as all the stars.
Vibrant Christmas lights
dancing on the potent pine tree.
Carol singers in the background.
Delicate snowflakes land on the ground
peacefully in the chilly air.
In the warmth, heat travels around comforting me.
Sleepily, as my eyes start to close,
I go into hibernation for winter.

Georgie Arthur (11)
Wheatley CE Primary School, Wheatley

My Winter Wonderland

First, take a pinch of a season,
Morning mist creeping around the village.
The stars are glooming on the white snow,
Go outside and make the best snow angels.
Gather your closest family and friends,
And have a festive feast.
Next, have a massive snowball fight,
Sprinkle glitter on the snow.
Get cosy next to the fire,
Now have a hot chocolate with marshmallows.

Brecon S
Wheatley CE Primary School, Wheatley

Winter

First, pick up the soft snow and make a snowman,
with the scarf and mittens,
Next, grab some hot chocolate with melted
marshmallows and cream.
Then, wrap the presents for your nearest
and dearest ready to go under the tree,
After, make your favourite Christmas dinner
and put it on the table.
Then, go outside with the warm clothes
and enjoy Christmas time.

Uliana Dubinina (11)
Wheatley CE Primary School, Wheatley

Tomato Soup

Happily, gobbled up.
As warm as lava, the soup boiled.
The soup boiled, belly rumbled, soup cooking.
As creamy as whipped cream.
As warm as a campfire.
As tasty as heaven.
My belly is as loud as a volcano.
In a bowl waiting to be in my belly.
My tomato soup is boiling, belly rumbling.
As creamy as whipped cream.
My belly is as loud as a volcano!

Archie Hawkins (11)
Wheatley CE Primary School, Wheatley

Winter

Winter calling,
Freezing falling,
Icicles forming,
Water freezing,
Frost branching,
Beautifully glistening,
Ice smashing,
Snowballs flying,
Fires warming,
Smoke rising,
Snow crunching,
Snowflakes landing,
Sparkling twinkling,
Animals hibernating,
Robins cheeping,
Morning coming,
Sun rising,
Spring arriving.

Aaron Lomas (10)
Wheatley CE Primary School, Wheatley

My Snowy Winter

A snowman next to a snowdome,
Children gathering snowballs
around the snowing stars.
Adults are watching with a cup of cocoa
Families snowboarding around the snowing hills.
Icy ballerinas dancing around the ice.
People are watching 'Snowman and the Snowdog'
The fires are smoking and hot chocolate steaming.
Trees moving with the ice and snow.

Valentina (10)
Wheatley CE Primary School, Wheatley

Fireplace

Mildly, stunningly, crackling, glistening,
Burning as brightly as the midday sun.
A supply of light, sitting, glowing,
Filling the room like a firework.
I see it flicker,
Rapidly, wildly and fast.
The flame is swaying,
But slowly fading,
Like taking one last bow.
The family is here,
Wanting its warmth,
On this cold winter night.

Noah Tuppenney (11)
Wheatley CE Primary School, Wheatley

How To Make The Best Christmas Spell

First, sprinkle a little bit of sparkling hot chocolate
powder, and pour in some Christmas spirit.
Go outside in the glittering snow,
Make snow angels with laughter and fun.

Come inside for a nice Christmas feast,
And finish it off with a lovely winter's nap.

Gather your friends for a special treat,
Put your feet up nice and neat.

Samuel C (10)
Wheatley CE Primary School, Wheatley

Winter

Amazing, wonderful,
Thick, glistening, beautiful snow,
Sparkling in the lights that glow,
Happy, laughing, children playing,
They wish it was forever staying,
Delicious, warm pudding as sweet as toffee,
Parents sit down enjoying their boiling coffee,
Soft, silky, cosy blankets keeping them warm,
Everyone is safe from the blazing winter storm.

Henry (10)

Wheatley CE Primary School, Wheatley

Snow

Quickly, joyfully, glazing, swaying,
The icy frosty grass brushes against my feet,
Bouncing like a rabbit to get warm in the ice cold,
The misty mist mirrors the window,
The warm blanket covers me.
Listening to the children play,
I'm sipping on my hot chocolate,
Wondering about the new adventures
that wait for me in the year coming ahead.

Lizzie Webb (11)
Wheatley CE Primary School, Wheatley

Winter Season

Firstly gather your friends and family
for a nice winter's walk,
Watch the icicles sparkling from the frozen tree.
Watch your hot breath make a cloud of smoke,
Then wrap your scarf around your neck.
Once home put logs on the burning fire,
And snuggle up in your favourite blanket
while you enjoy the soft, velvety chocolate
melts in your mouth.

Eren K (10)
Wheatley CE Primary School, Wheatley

Sledging

Going down a covered hill of fluffy snow,
Kids shout and scream
when they slide down the hill,
Some people are satisfied by the ice shattering
into one hundred specs of twinkling ice.
Snow falls,
Sometimes it gets heavy.
Very heavy.
Too heavy.
They must go home inside to the warmth
with the snow still raging on.

Joshua Lindsay (11)
Wheatley CE Primary School, Wheatley

Snowman

Happily, silently, throwing, making
As cold as a freezer -10°
Like a snowman falling through the sky gracefully
Gracefully, the snowman feels the frozen touch
land on his white soft fingers
The snowman on top of the hill
illuminated by the light
Snowman is lonely and lost bright,
so bright on a white wintery stage.

Jacob Banas (10)
Wheatley CE Primary School, Wheatley

Frost

Building, drifting
The icicle with freezing water cracked
Clouds as white as anything
with snow slowly falling from the sky
As Christmas crackers are pulled,
I smell the scrumptious turkey cooking in the oven.
Each delicate dancer is illuminated by the blinding
midday sun making it like a spotlight.

Ebony Marlow (11)
Wheatley CE Primary School, Wheatley

Hot Chocolate

Warm yummy, cosy, comforting.
A perfect hot chocolate, as warm as a hot tub.
Steam warm like the sun.
I smell the cinnamon air racing around my room.
The smell is like heaven.
The fire lit all snug and cosy.
I feel the warm air all around me,
as I sip my drink snuggled up in a blanket.

Ronnie Bolton (9)
Wheatley CE Primary School, Wheatley

Snowmen

Joyfully, standing, excitedly, sparkling,
Standing as still as a statue,
The icy frozen statue standing in the night.
On a majestic hill,
Bells were ringing,
Carollers singing,
Winter is here.
Now we cheer,
For winter.
Snow sparkling,
The winter feeling is here.

Lewis P (11)
Wheatley CE Primary School, Wheatley

Fairy Lights

Twinkly, sparkly, decorating,
Fairy lights as colourful as a rainbow,
Shining magically and brightly.
Shimmering twinkling fairy lights
hung up and down the streets.
Flashing and shining all around,
Bright, glistening, twinkling, shining.
Shining like the sun.

Jasmine Cook (10)
Wheatley CE Primary School, Wheatley

Snow

Gracefully covering gardens,
making white fluffy blankets,
Snow falling onto me, making me into a snowman,
Presents wrapped as colourfully as rainbows,
Juiciest turkey you have ever tasted,
The smell of bonfires and smoke,
Crisp white snow I stumbled upon.

Darcy Normington (10)
Wheatley CE Primary School, Wheatley

Snowflakes

As I am playing in the snow,
Opening presents recklessly,
My brother slowly opens them.
Snowflakes fly as they catch the sky,
Flying,
Sliding down.
I see the turkey,
I taste the turkey,
I smell the turkey,
The flakes stay in place.

Lewis Robins (9)
Wheatley CE Primary School, Wheatley

Sledge

Excitedly, quickly, twirling, gliding,
Falling as gracefully as an ice skater.
Ice skater gliding, falling, floating
Making me laugh whilst going down the hill.
Crunch! The ice is breaking underfoot
As I take one last sledge down the hill.

Niamh Nichols (10)
Wheatley CE Primary School, Wheatley

Snowflakes

Gracefully, beautifully, twinkling, glittering,
Flying as magically as winter fairies.
Fairies, singing, glistening, floating,
The gentle, graceful, flakes
floating onto my tongue.
Silently landing on the ground
like a pinch of winter magic.

Constance Prentice (9)
Wheatley CE Primary School, Wheatley

Children

Happily, comfortingly, snowing, playing,
Hugging family as tightly as a wrapped present,
Hearing children laughing with joy.
Hot chocolate is as calming
as watching night stars,
The bright white snowball splatted on the window
As if a fly.

Lenny Davies (10)
Wheatley CE Primary School, Wheatley

Snow

Gently falling like a drop of rain,
Twirling ballerinas dancing.
So cold that it hurts my hands.
Creamy hot chocolate warming my hands.
Everywhere is white,
Snowflakes glide like birds in the sky,
I watch the snow gliding through the sky.

Zoyia Zaidi (10)
Wheatley CE Primary School, Wheatley

Snow

Gracefully, nicely, falling, snowing.
Falling as gracefully as a ballerina on pointe,
Ballerinas dancing in the sky.
I can hear the gentle snowflakes fall
as the ballerinas dance gracefully,
Keeping me warm with my boiling hot chocolate.

Poppy Collins (10)
Wheatley CE Primary School, Wheatley

Children

Happily, excitedly, laughing, talking,
Laughing as loud as a siren.
Children dancing, happily, loudly,
Snoring, sneezing, smoky fireplace.
Each little kid opening presents with joy,
Happy, so happy,
Cheer, cheer,
Final gift!

Klevis (10)
Wheatley CE Primary School, Wheatley

Snowflakes

Feathers fell lightly, skimming the ground.
Floating down, planting themselves on my tongue.
Frosty flakes, glistening.
Sun striking my eyes, imitating a radiator.
Snow is melting in my mouth,
feeling like a piece of candyfloss.

William (10)
Wheatley CE Primary School, Wheatley

Snowflakes

Recklessly, sparkly, falling, settling,
Sticking as tightly as glue.
I hear the crunch under my feet
of fresh fallen snow,
The snow illuminates a path,
Leading me to treasure.
The dancing snowflakes are a magical daydream.

Gabriella Rhoades-Brown (9)
Wheatley CE Primary School, Wheatley

Snow

The glimmering light shining through the window
The snow falling to the ground
The ice melts down the road
Freezing cold ice melting away,
sledging down the hill
Twinkling, flashing, lighting up the tree.

Robyn Lyne
Wheatley CE Primary School, Wheatley

Snowflakes

Falling from the sky,
Watching them delighted, as they float by.
Wondering why winter, comes and goes away.
Waiting for Santa to come another day.
Excited children in the snow,
Watching the lights glow.

Rosie Somers (11)
Wheatley CE Primary School, Wheatley

Hot Chocolate

Warm, tasty storm of flavour,
Warmer than my blanket.
Hot like fire.
Guaranteed to blow your mind with flavour.
It gives me the stuff I need and same with you.

Zac (9)
Wheatley CE Primary School, Wheatley

Snowballs

Recklessly, quickly, floating, throwing
Flying as fast as an aeroplane.
Crashing, breaking.

Bobby-Ross Doyle (9)
Wheatley CE Primary School, Wheatley

YoungWriters Est. 1991

Young Writers Information

We hope you have enjoyed reading this book – and that you will continue to in the coming years.

If you're the parent or family member of an enthusiastic poet or story writer, do visit our website **www.youngwriters.co.uk/subscribe** and sign up to receive news, competitions, writing challenges and tips, activities and much, much more! There's lots to keep budding writers motivated!

If you would like to order further copies of this book, or any of our other titles, then please give us a call or order via your online account.

Young Writers
Remus House
Coltsfoot Drive
Peterborough
PE2 9BF
(01733) 890066
info@youngwriters.co.uk

Join in the conversation!
Tips, news, giveaways and much more!

YoungWritersUK **YoungWritersCW**
youngwriterscw **youngwriterscw**